Editor
Janine Amos
Designer
Winsome Malcolm

Series Adviser
Betty Root
Tutor in Charge
Centre for the Teaching of Reading
Reading University School of Education

ISBN 0 361 05380 0
Copyright © 1982 Purnell Publishers Limited
Published 1982 by Purnell Books, Paulton, Bristol, BS18 5LQ
Made and printed in Great Britain by
Purnell and Sons (Book Production) Limited, Paulton, Bristol

Counting

Illustrated by
Pamela Storey

PURNELL

1 2 3 4 5

one fox running

6 7 8 9 10

1 2 3 4 5

two horses jumping

6 7 8 9 10

three lambs skipping

6 7 8 9 10

1 2 3 4 5

four birds flying

6 7 8 9 10

1 2 3 4 5

five rabbits hopping

6 7 8 9 10

1 2 3 4 5

six babies sleeping

6 7 8 9 10

1 2 3 4 5

seven pigs eating

6 7 8 9 10

1 2 3 4 5

eight goldfish swimming

6 7 8 9 10

1 2 3 4 5

nine dogs barking

6 7 8 9 10

1 2 3 4 5

ten children playing

6 7 8 9 10

One, two, three, four, five,
Once I caught a fish alive .

Six, seven, eight, nine, ten,
Then I let him go again!